THE LUMINEER
FOR UKULELE

Front cover ukulele photo courtesy of Flight Instruments

ISBN 978-1-5400-8437-8

Visit Hal Leonard Online at
www.halleonard.com

Contact us:
Hal Leonard
7777 West Bluemound Road
Milwaukee, WI 53213
Email: info@halleonard.com

In Europe, contact:
Hal Leonard Europe Limited
42 Wigmore Street
Marylebone, London, W1U 2RN
Email: info@halleonardeurope.com

In Australia, contact:
Hal Leonard Australia Pty. Ltd.
4 Lentara Court
Cheltenham, Victoria, 3192 Australia
Email: info@halleonard.com.au

Angela

Words and Music by Jeremy Fraites, Wesley Schultz and Simone Felice

First note

Verse

Driving Folk beat

1. When you left this ___ town ___ with your win - dows ___ down ___ and the
(2.) Vol - vo ___ lights ___ lit up green and ___ white ___ with the

wil - der - ness ___ in - side.
cit - ies on ___ the signs.

Let the ex - its ___ pass, ___ all the
But you held your ___ course ___ to some

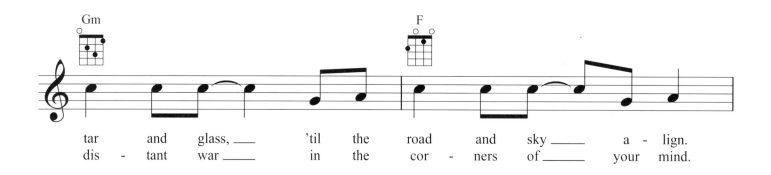

tar and glass, ___ 'til the road and sky ___ a - lign.
dis - tant war ___ in the cor - ners of ___ your mind.

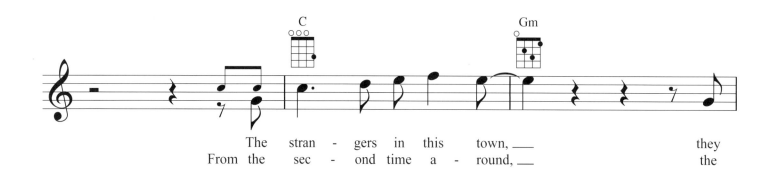

The stran - gers in this town, ___ they
From the sec - ond time a - round, ___ the

raise you up _____ just to cut you down. _____ Oh, An -
on - ly love _____ I _____ ev - er found. _____ Oh, An -

\- ge - la, it's a long time com - ing. _____
\- ge - la, it's a long time com - ing. _____

1.   **2.**   **Interlude**

2. And your   Home at last. _____

_____   3. Were you

Verse

safe and __ warm __ in your coat of ___ arms __ with your

fin - gers in _____ a fist?   Did you

hear the ___ notes, ___ all those stat - ic codes ___ in the

ra - di - o ___ a - byss? The stran - gers in this town, ___

___ they raised you up ___ just to cut you down. ___ Oh, An -

- ge - la, it's a long time com - ing. _____

Oh, An - ge - la, spent your whole life run - ning a - way.

%. Chorus

Home at last. _____

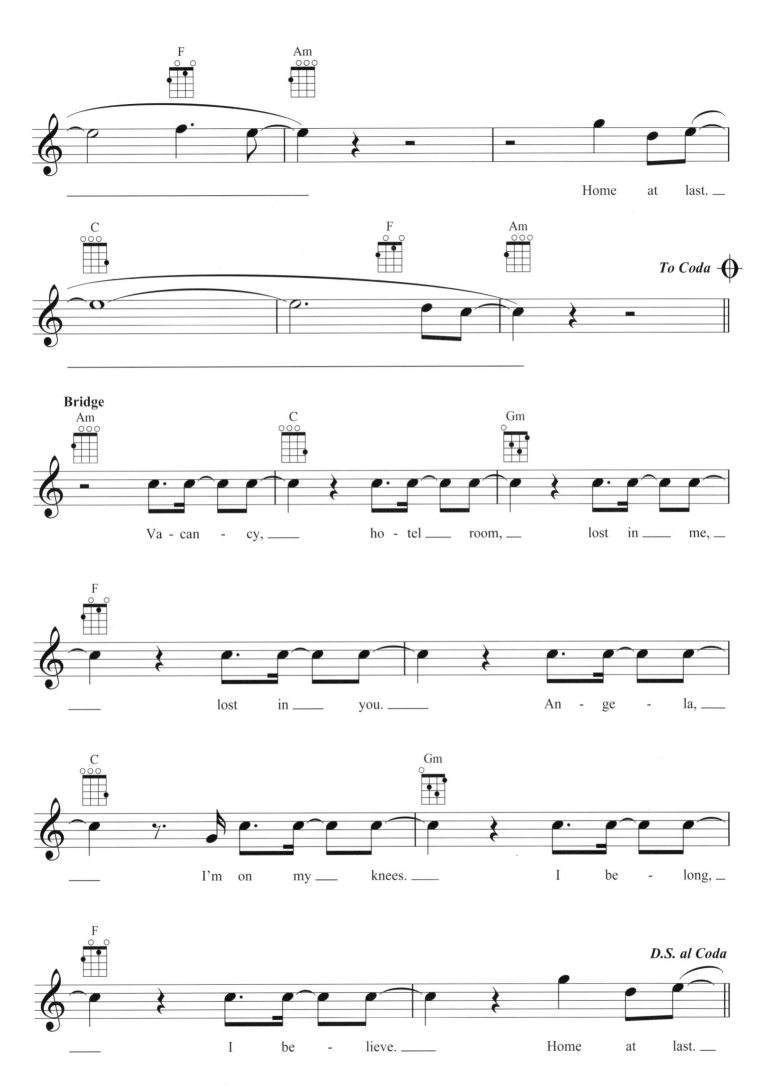

Home at last. __

To Coda ⊕

Bridge

Va - can - cy, ____ ho - tel __ room, __ lost in ____ me, __

____ lost in ____ you. ____ An - ge - la, ___

____ I'm on my ___ knees. ___ I be - long, __

D.S. al Coda

____ I be - lieve. ____ Home at last. __

Gloria

Words and Music by Jeremy Fraites and Wesley Schultz

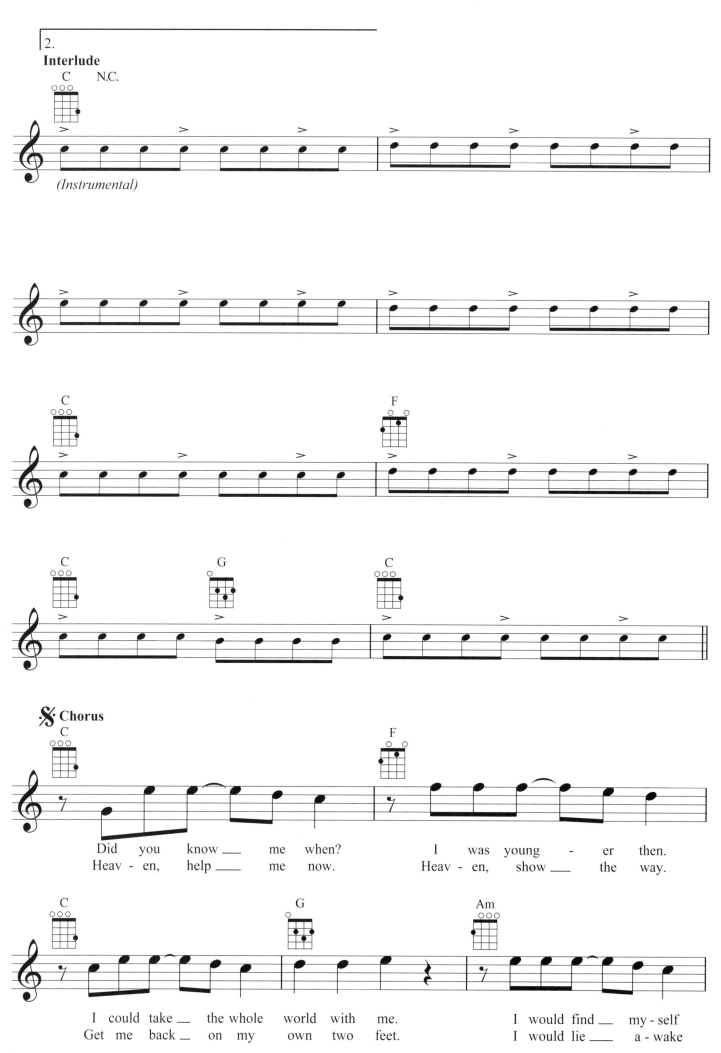

Did you know ___ me when? I was young - er then.
Heav - en, help ___ me now. Heav - en, show ___ the way.

I could take ___ the whole world with me. I would find ___ my-self
Get me back ___ on my own two feet. I would lie ___ a - wake

feel-in' a - lone, ____ oh. ____
and pray __ you don't lie a - wake for me. ____

Heav - en, help __ me now. Heav - en, show __ the way.
Ev - 'ry night __ a - wake, ev - 'ry day __ a - lone. } Get me back __ on my

own two feet. I would lie ___ a - wake ___ and pray __ you don't

lie a - wake for me. Oh, __

Bridge

__ oh, ____ oh, ____ oh.

oh, ____ oh, __ oh.

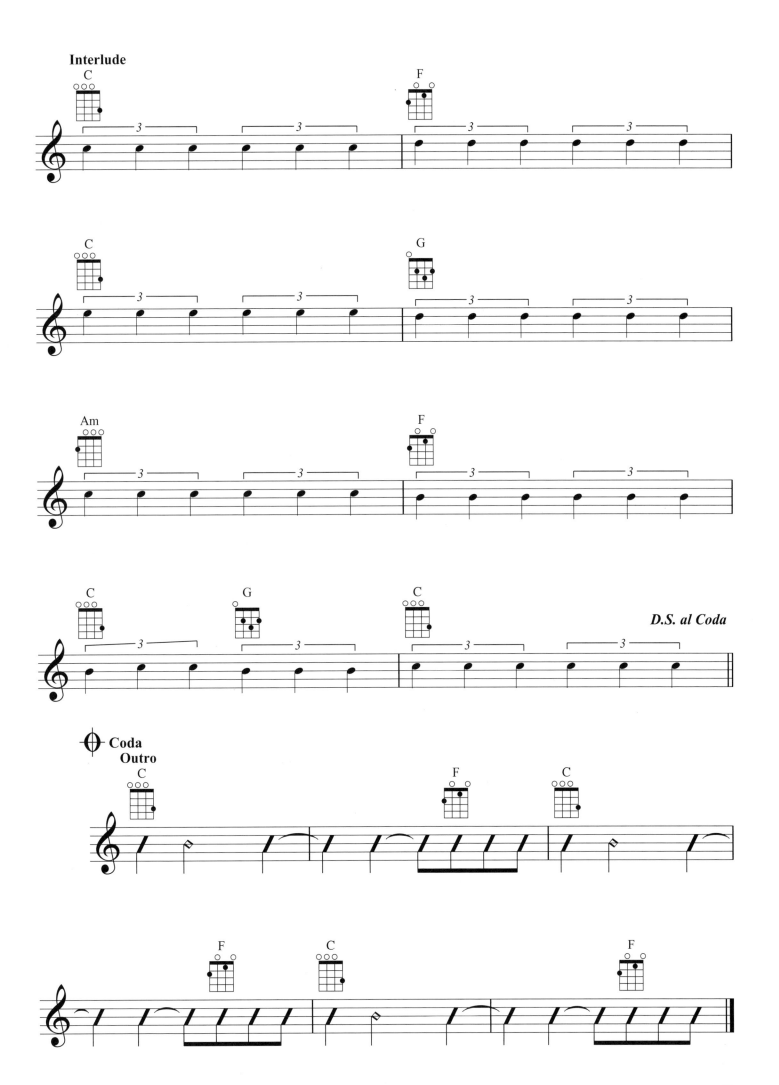

Cleopatra

Words and Music by Jeremy Fraites, Wesley Schultz and Simone Felice

1. I was Cle - o - pat - ra, I was young and an ac -

- tress, when you knelt by my mat - tress and asked for my

hand. But I was sad. You asked __

__ it as I laid in a black __ dress, with my

fa - ther in a cas - ket. I had no plans, __

yeah. _____

Verse

2. And I left the foot - prints, the mud stained on the car - pet. And it hard - ened like my heart _____ did when you left town. ___ But I must ad - mit it, that I would mar - ry you ___ in an in - stant. Damn your wife, ___ I'd be your mis - tress just to have you a -

Chorus

round.   But I was   late   for   this, __   late   for   that. __

Late   for   the   love __   of   my ___ life. __   And   when   I   die   a - lone, __   when   I

die   a - lone, __   die   I'll   be   on   time. ___

let chord ring

Ahh. _____

Verse

3. And   while   the   church   dis - cour - aged   an - y   lust __

___   that   burned   with - in _____ me,   yes,   my   flesh, ___   it   was   not   cur -

ren - cy but I held true. _____ So I

drive a tax - i, and the traf - fic _____ dis - tracts _____

_____ me from the stran - gers in my back _____ seat. They re - mind me of

Chorus

you. But I was late for this,

late for that. Late for the love _____ of my _____ life. _____ And when I

To Coda

die a - lone, _____ when I _____ die a - lone, when I die, I'll be on time. _____

Bridge

The on - ly gifts from my Lord __

__ were birth and a di - vorce.

But I've read this script __ and the cos - tume __ fits, __

so I'll play __ my part. ____

Verse

4. I was Cle - o - pat -

- ra, I was tall - er than the raft - ers. But that's

Donna

Words and Music by Jeremy Fraites and Wesley Schultz

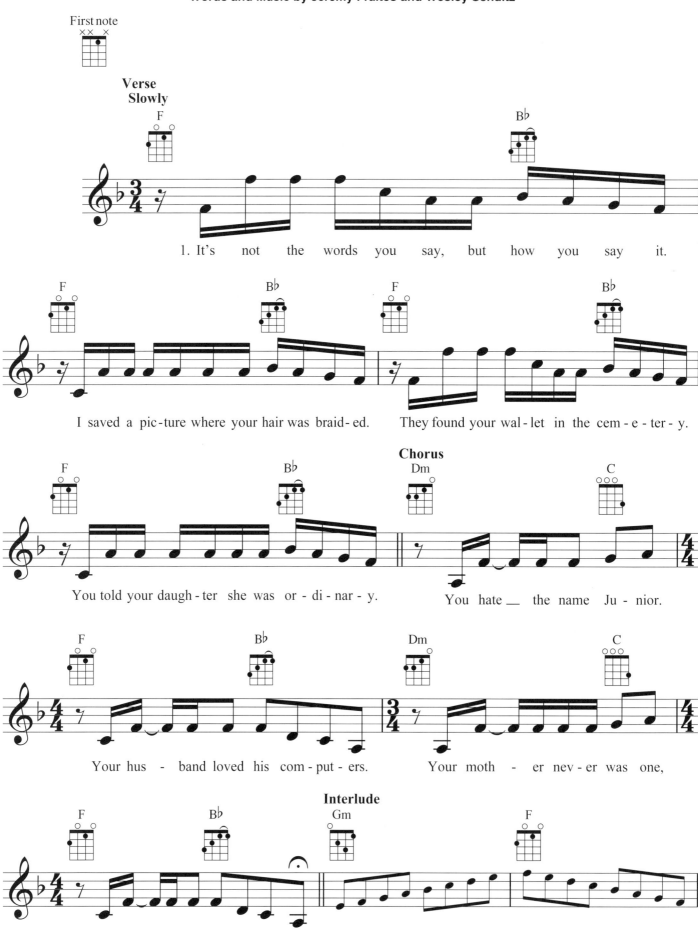

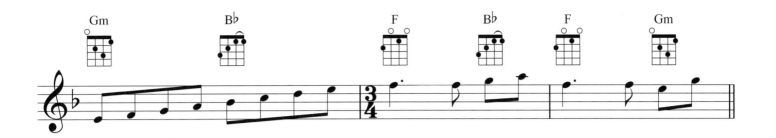

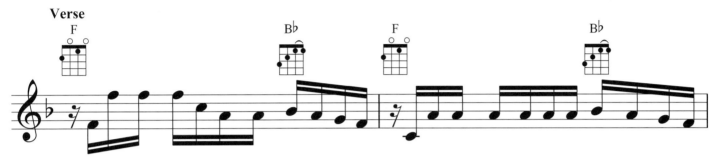

Verse

2. If you don't have it, then you'll nev-er give it.   And I don't blame you for the way you're liv-ing.

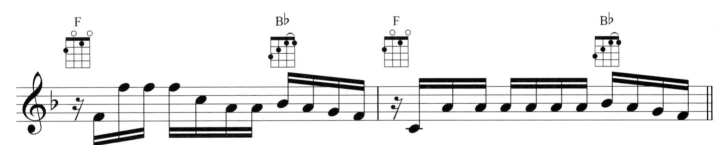

A lit-tle boy was born in Feb-ru-ar-y.   You could-n't so-ber up to hold a ba-by.

Chorus

You hate __ the name Don-na.   You love __ to judge stran-gers' kar-ma.

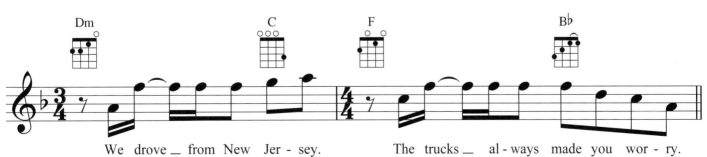

We drove __ from New Jer-sey.   The trucks __ al-ways made you wor-ry.

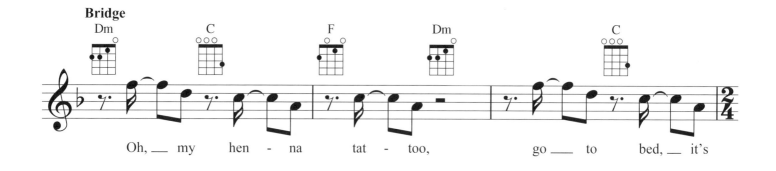

Bridge

Oh, __ my hen - na tat - too, go __ to bed, __ it's

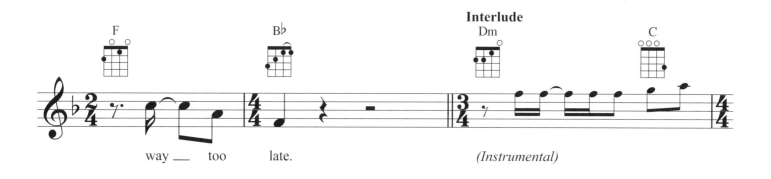

Interlude

way __ too late. *(Instrumental)*

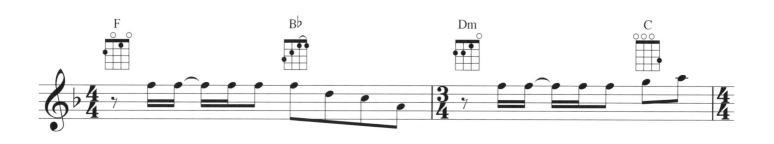

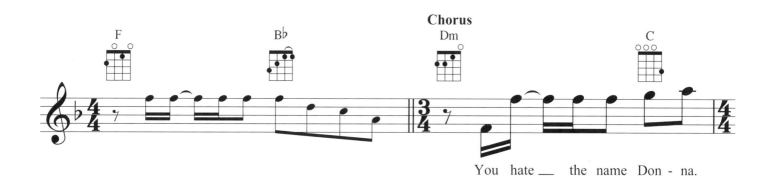

Chorus

You hate __ the name Don - na.

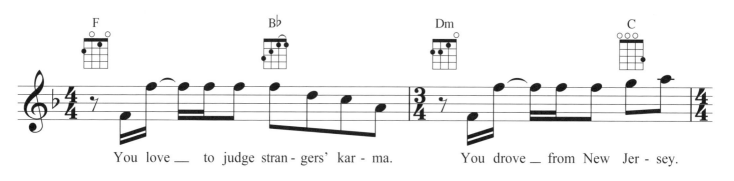

You love __ to judge stran - gers' kar - ma. You drove __ from New Jer - sey.

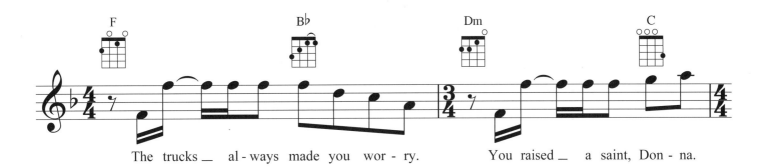

The trucks _ al - ways made you wor - ry. You raised _ a saint, Don - na.

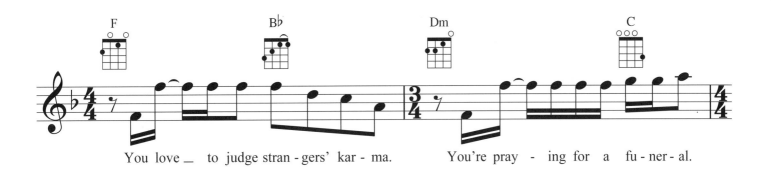

You love _ to judge stran - gers' kar - ma. You're pray - ing for a fu - ner - al.

Outro

You're sing - ing like Hal - le - lu - jah. You're sing - ing like Hal - le - lu - jah.

You're sing - ing like Hal - le - lu - jah. You're sing - ing like Hal - le - lu - jah. _

You're sing - ing like Hal - le - lu - jah. _____

Flapper Girl

Words and Music by Jeremy Fraites and Wesley Schultz

First note

Verse
With a lilt

1. Cut off all _____ of your hair. _____
4. Ro - me - o, _____ Ju - li - et,

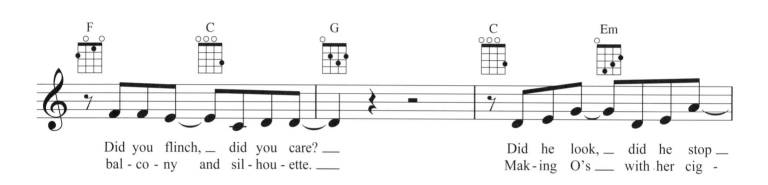

Did you flinch, _ did you care? _____
bal - co - ny and sil - hou - ette. _____

Did he look, _ did he stop
Mak - ing O's _ with her cig -

_____ and _ stare _____ at your brand - new hair? _____
- a - rette, _____ it's _ Ju - li - et. _____

Verse

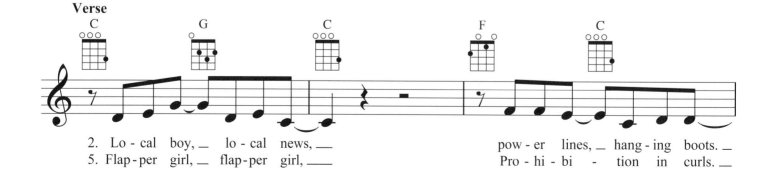

2. Lo - cal boy, _ lo - cal news, _ pow - er lines, _ hang - ing boots. _
5. Flap - per girl, _ flap - per girl, _____ Pro - hi - bi - tion in curls. _

Fi - re - men — in their trucks — cut — loose —
Hair of gold — and a neck — of — pearls, —

To Coda

Verse

a lo - cal boy's shoes. —
it's flap - per girl. —

3. Cad - il - lac, — Cad - il - lac, —

bus' - ness men — dressed in slacks. —

I will buy — one for us — when I — get back, — a big Cad - il - lac. —

Pre-Chorus

And you can wave to all — your friends, — and I'll nev -

Chorus

- er leave — you a - gain. —

Would you write, — would you call

back, ba - by, if _____ I wrote you a song? ___

___ I've been gone, ___ but you're still ___

___ my la - dy and _____ I need you at home. ___

D.C. al Coda

___

Coda

___ And you can

Pre-Chorus

wave to all _____ of your friends, ___ and I'll nev -
ain't be - hind ___ my ___ door, ___ then I ain't ___

- er leave ___ you a - gain. ___ }
___ got a home ___ an - y - more. ___ }

24

Flowers in Your Hair

Words and Music by Jeremy Fraites and Wesley Schultz

Gale Song

Words and Music by Jeremy Fraites, Wesley Schultz and Neyla Pekarek

And I don't want to go, but it's time ___ to

leave. You'll be on my ___ mind, ___ in my

Chorus

des - ti - ny. And I won't

fight in vain. ___ I love you

just the same. ___ Ooh. ___ I could - n't know ___

___ what's in your mind. ___

30

Outro

Ho Hey

Words and Music by Jeremy Fraites and Wesley Schultz

Additional Lyrics

2. (Ho!) So show me, family,
   (Hey!) All the blood that I will bleed.
   (Ho!) I don't know where I belong,
   (Hey!) I don't know where I went wrong,
   (Ho!) But I can write a song.
   (Hey!)

3. (Ho!) I don't think you're right for him.
   (Hey!) Look at what it might have been if you
   (Ho!) Took a bus to Chinatown.
   (Hey!) I'd be standing on Canal
   (Ho!) And Bowery. *(To Coda 1)*

It Wasn't Easy to Be Happy for You

Words and Music by Jeremy Fraites and Wesley Schultz

You held your punch-es back, and I left the room. Yeah, ___ it was-n't

1.
eas - y to be hap - py for you. ___

2.
2. All a - lone, ___ eas - y to be hap - py for you.

Bridge
I know ___ that you tried, ___ but you're no ___ friend of mine. ___

___ Fall - ing a - part, ___ you played ___ it the best, ___ a dame ___ in dis - tress. ___

Chorus
Yeah, ___ it was - n't
Yeah, ___ it was - n't

Life in the City

Words and Music by Jeremy Fraites and Wesley Schultz

2. And if you leave, __ don't leave me all a-lone; __

_____ 'cause I'll be scared, ____ I'll be na-ked, I'll get cold.

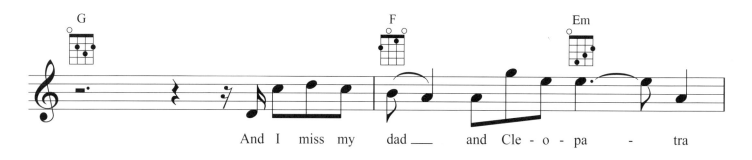

And I miss my dad ___ and Cle-o-pa - tra

sit-ting on the phone. __ So take me back _____ off these __ streets, and we'll

nev - er be a-part, __ to-geth - er from the start, __

D.S. al Coda

nev - er, nev - er fall - ing back a - lone. __ Whoa __ whoa, __

Coda

Bridge-Outro

And if the sun don't shine on me to-da da da da da da

day, and if the sub-ways flood and bridg-es
da. Da da da da da da da da

break, will you just lay down and dig your
da. Da da da

grave? Or will you rail a-gainst your dy - ing

day? Da da da da da da da da

da. Da da da da da da da da da.

41

Ophelia

Words and Music by Jeremy Fraites and Wesley Schultz

First note

Verse

Moderate half-time feel, with a strong beat

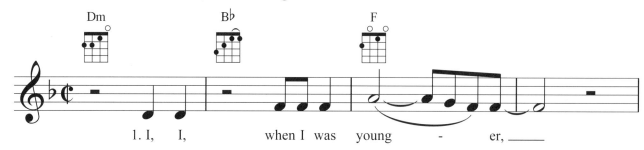

1. I, I, when I was young - er, ___

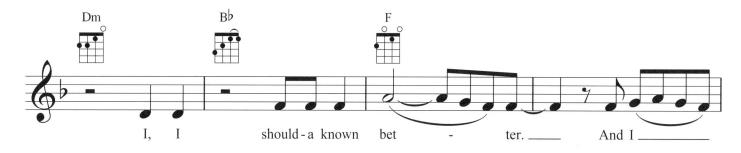

I, I should - a known bet - ter. ___ And I ___

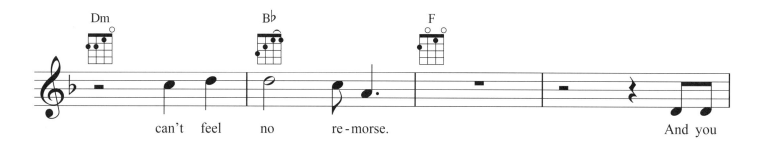

can't feel no re - morse. And you

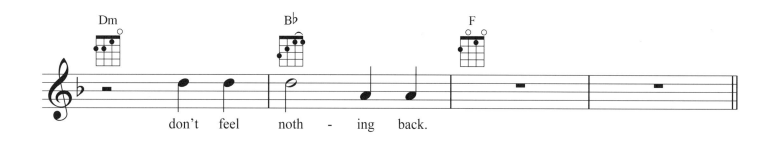

don't feel noth - ing back.

Interlude

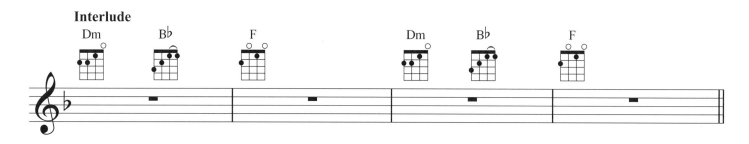

Salt and the Sea

Words and Music by Jeremy Fraites and Wesley Schultz

1. Could it be I _____ was the one _____ that you held _____ so deep _____ in the night? _____ On the back stair - - case you fell _____ to your knees _____ with tears _____ in your eyes. _____ All that you suf - fered, all the dis - ease, _____ you could - n't _____ hide _____ it, hide it from me. _____ 2. All a - lone, scared _____

in your room, _____ would you swear _____ there's no - bod - y home? _____
these pre - scrip - tions, they wrote _____ me off _____ like a heel. _____

On the bed, lay -
Yeah, the doc - tors _____

- in' a - wake _____ as you prayed, _____ he'd leave _____ you a - lone. _____
with their med - i - cine left _____ me to rock in my filth. _____

I'll let the dark - ness swal - low me whole. _____
From the de - struc - tion, out of the flame. _____

I need to find _____ you, need you to know. _____
You need a vil - lain, give me a name. _____

Chorus

I'll be your friend ___ in the day-

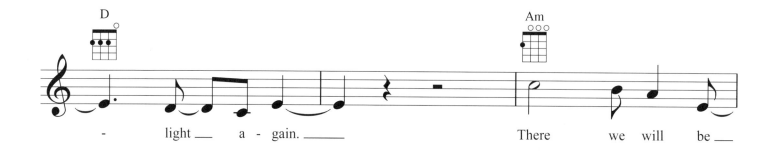

- light ___ a - gain. _____ There we will be ___

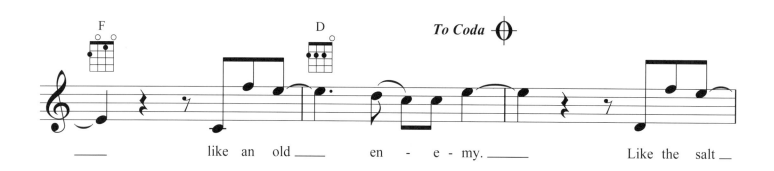

___ like an old ___ en - e - my. _____ Like the salt ___

Interlude

___ and ___ the sea. _____

D.S. al Coda

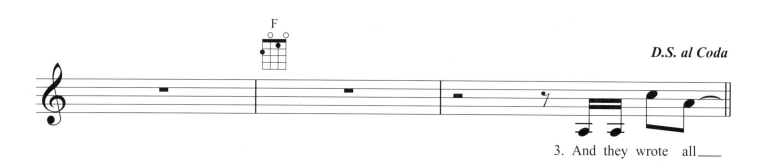

3. And they wrote all___

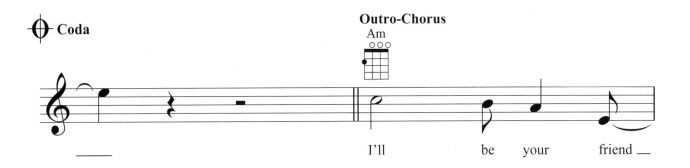

Coda

Outro-Chorus

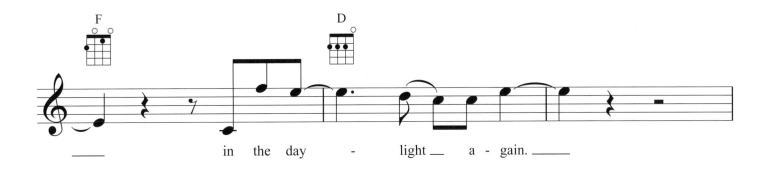

I'll be your friend ___

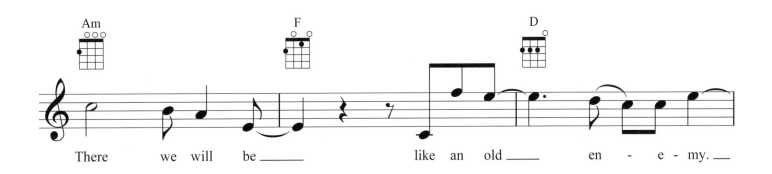

___ in the day - light ___ a - gain. _____

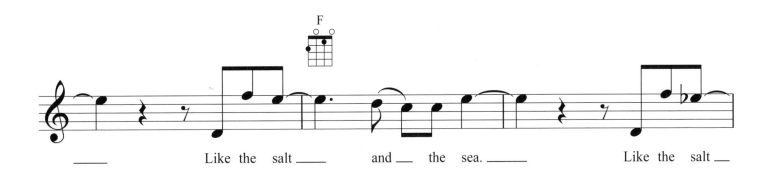

There we will be _____ like an old _____ en - e - my. __

___ Like the salt _____ and ___ the sea. _____ Like the salt __

and ___ the sea. _____

Stubborn Love

Words and Music by Jeremy Fraites and Wesley Schultz

First note

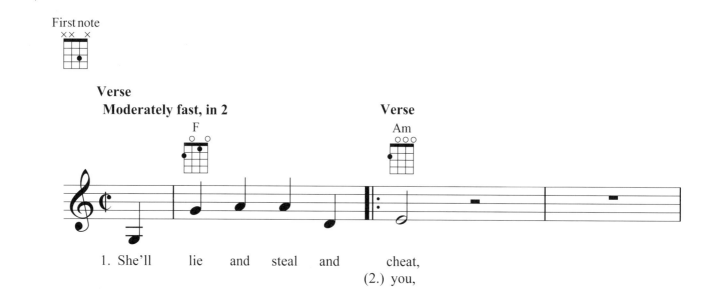

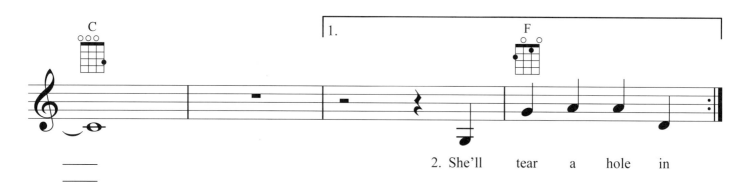

noth - ing at all. _____

The op - po - site of love's in - dif -

- fer - ence. _____ So

pay at - ten - tion, now; I'm

stand - ing on your porch scream - ing out, ____

____ and I won't leave un - til you come ____

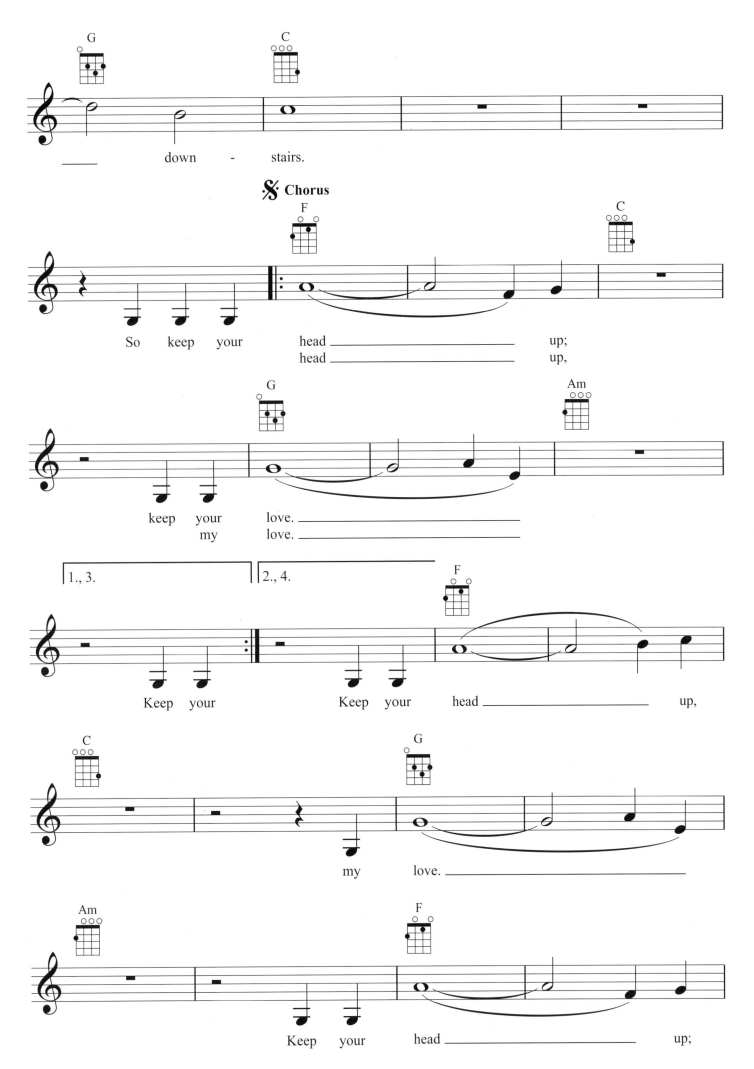

keep your love. _____

To Coda ⊕

4. And I _____ don't blame _ you,

Verse

dear,
(5.) close,

for run - ning like you
but I don't read those

did all _____ these years. _____
things an - y - more. _____

I would do the
I nev - er trust - ed

same, you'd best _____ be - lieve. _____
my _____ own _____ eyes. _____

1.

2.

5. The high - way signs _ say we're

Submarines

Words and Music by Jeremy Fraites and Wesley Schultz

First note

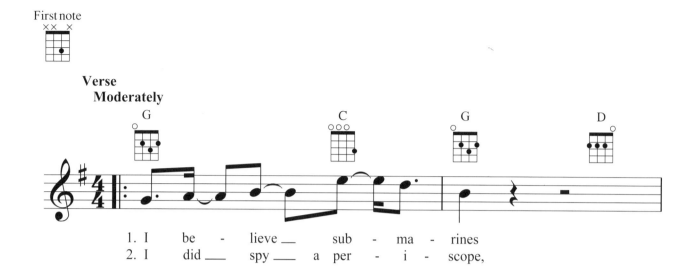

Verse
Moderately

1. I be - lieve ___ sub - ma - rines
2. I did ___ spy ___ a per - i - scope,

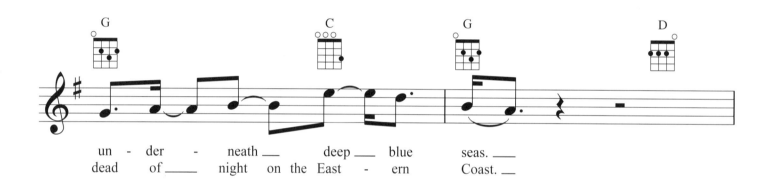

un - der - neath ___ deep ___ blue seas. ___
dead of ___ night on the East - ern Coast. ___

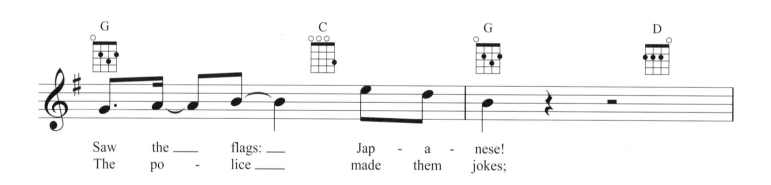

Saw the ___ flags: ___ Jap - a - nese!
The po - lice ___ made them jokes;

No one ___ will ___ be - lieve me. ___
told me ___ I'd ___ seen ___ a ghost. ___

Chorus

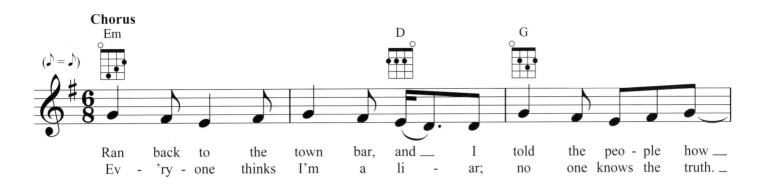

Ran back to the town bar, and ___ I told the peo - ple how ___
Ev - 'ry - one thinks I'm a li - ar; no one knows the truth. _

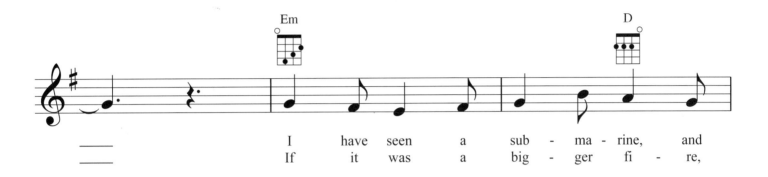

___ I have seen a sub - ma - rine, and
___ If it was a big - ger fi - re,

1.

ev - 'ry - one laughed a - loud. _____
I would be

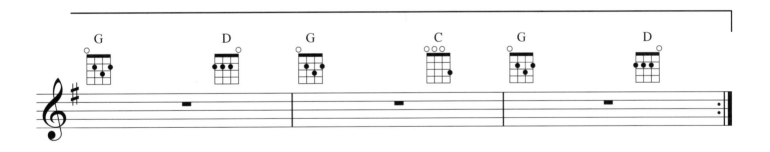

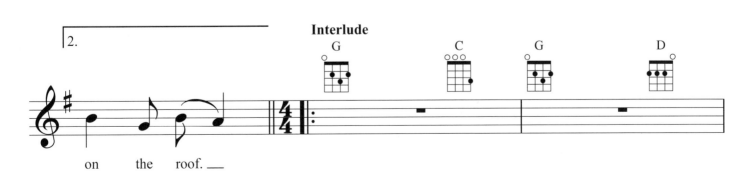

Interlude

2.

on the roof. ___

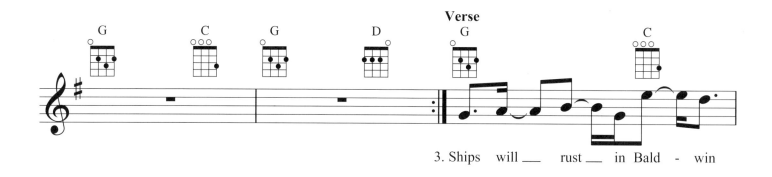

3. Ships will __ rust __ in Bald - win

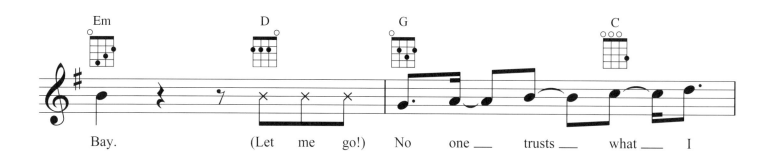

Bay.   (Let me go!)   No   one __ trusts __ what __ I

say.   (I don't know!)   Oh   my __ God, __ no __ one

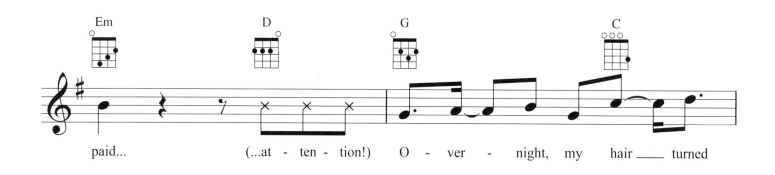

paid...   (...at - ten - tion!)   O - ver - night, my hair __ turned

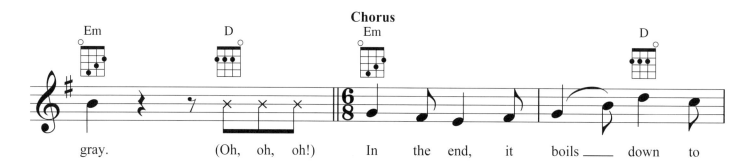

gray.   (Oh, oh, oh!)   In   the end, it boils __ down to

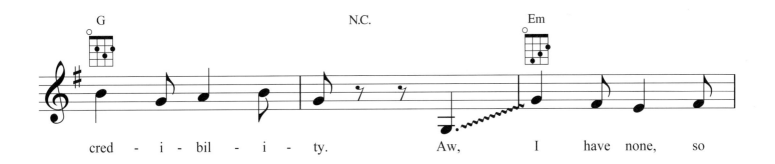

cred - i - bil - i - ty.   Aw,   I   have   none,   so

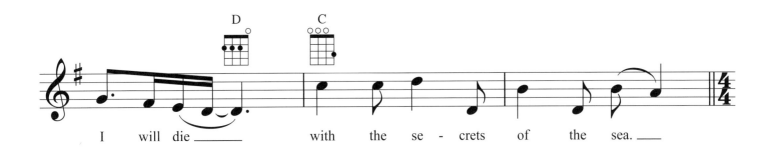

I   will   die _____   with   the   se - crets   of   the   sea. ___

Outro

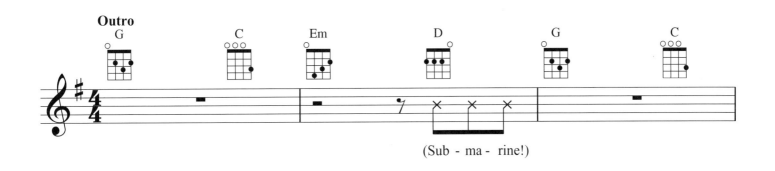

(Sub - ma - rine!)

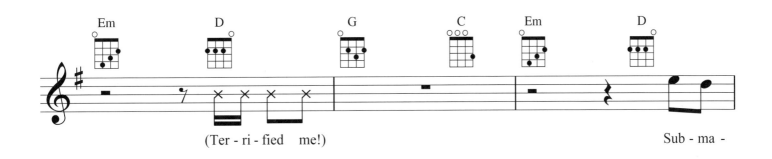

(Ter - ri - fied   me!)   Sub - ma -

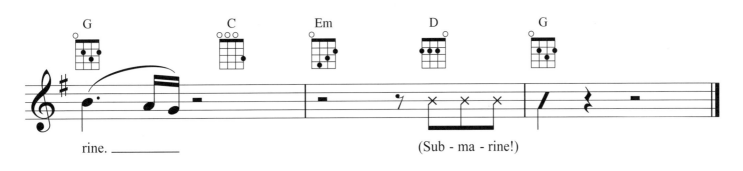

rine. _____   (Sub - ma - rine!)

Sleep on the Floor

Words and Music by Jeremy Fraites and Wesley Schultz

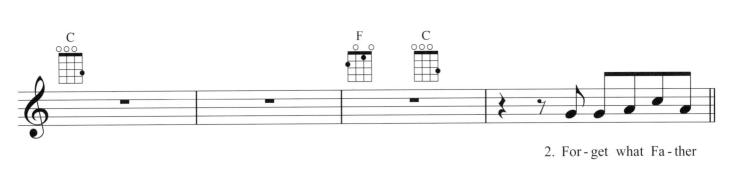

2. For - get what Fa - ther

Verse

Bren - nan said; _____ we were not born in sin. Leave a note

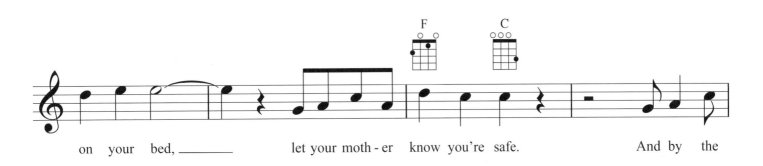

on your bed, _____ let your moth - er know you're safe. And by the

time she wakes, we'll have driv - en through the state,

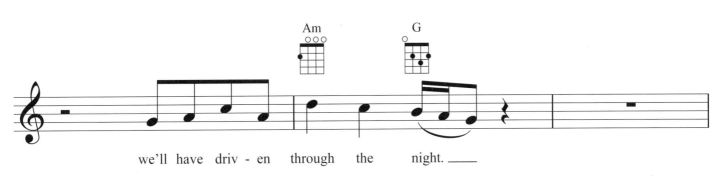

we'll have driv - en through the night. ____

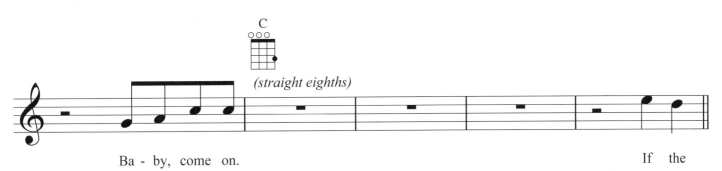

(straight eighths)

Ba - by, come on. If the

_____ on _____ us. _____   Oh, _____ Il - li - nois, _____

_____ Il - li - nois.

(swing eighths)

Outro-Verse

Pack your-self a tooth-brush, dear, _____ pack your-self a

fa - v'rite blouse.   Take a with-draw-al slip, _____

_____ take all of your sav - ings out.   'Cause if we don't

leave this town,   we might nev - er make it out. ___